# HOW TO LEARN ALMOST ANYTHING IN 48 HOURS

*BY*

*PETER HORSLEY*

Copyright © 2023 by Peter Horsley

All rights reserved. No part of this publication may be reproduced, distributed, or transmitted in any form or by any means, including photocopying, recording, or other electronic or mechanical methods, without the prior written permission of the publisher, except in the case of brief quotations embodied in critical reviews and certain other noncommercial uses permitted by copyright law.

# TABLE OF CONTENTS

**CHAPTER 1** .................................................. **6**

**THE POWER OF RAPID LEARNING** ....... **6**

   Debunking myths about learning capacities and time constraints ...................................... 7

   Success stories of rapid learning .................. 9

**CHAPTER 2** ................................................. **11**

**UNDERSTANDING YOUR LEARNING STYLE** ......................................................... **11**

   Self-assessment to determine your learning style ............................................................. 14

   Tailoring learning methods to fit your style . 17

**CHAPTER 3** ................................................. **20**

**SETTING CLEAR GOALS AND OBJECTIVES** ............................................. **20**

   How to define clear, achievable learning objectives .................................................... 23

   Techniques for maintaining focus and motivation ................................................... 26

**CHAPTER 4** ................................................. **30**

**TIME MANAGEMENT FOR EFFECTIVE LEARNING** ................................................ **30**

   Balancing learning with other life responsibilities ............................................ 33

Overcoming procrastination and distractions ....................................................................... 37

## CHAPTER 5 ................................................. 41
## MEMORY ENHANCEMENT TECHNIQUES ............................................. 41

Techniques to improve memory retention ... 44

Practice exercises for memory enhancement ....................................................................... 47

## CHAPTER 6 ................................................. 51
## CRITICAL THINKING AND UNDERSTANDING ...................................... 51

Techniques for deeper understanding of material ....................................................... 54

Applying knowledge in practical scenarios . 58

## CHAPTER 7 ................................................. 62
## ACCELERATING SKILL ACQUISITION 62

The role of practice and repetition ............... 65

Overcoming plateaus in skill development .. 69

## CHAPTER 8 ................................................. 73
## UTILIZING TECHNOLOGY AND RESOURCES ............................................... 73

Online courses, apps, and other digital aids . 76

Leveraging social networks and communities for learning .................................................. 79

**CHAPTER 9 ................................................. 83**

**HEALTH, WELLNESS, AND LEARNING 83**

Importance of sleep, nutrition, and exercise 85

Stress management techniques for optimal learning ...................................................... 87

**CHAPTER 10 ............................................. 90**

**MASTERING THE ART OF FOCUS AND CONCENTRATION ................................... 90**

Importance of a conducive learning environment ............................................... 92

Exercises and habits to enhance concentration for effective learning .................................. 95

The role of mindfulness and mental clarity in maintaining consistent focus ....................... 98

**CHAPTER 11 ........................................... 101**

**PUTTING IT ALL TOGETHER ............... 101**

Case studies and examples ........................ 104

Encouragement and advice for continued learning and growth .................................. 106

# CHAPTER 1

# THE POWER OF RAPID LEARNING

How to Learn almost anything in 48 Hours" is a book that opens up a new perspective on learning quickly and effectively. It is designed for anyone who wants to rapidly grasp new concepts or skills for professional advancement, academic success, or personal growth. The book discusses the misconception that rapid learning is a gift for only a few. It demonstrates that learning quickly is a skill that anyone can develop with the right approach and techniques.

The book emphasizes that learning isn't just about how much information you can cram into your brain in the shortest time. It's about understanding how you, as an individual, process information and how you can optimize this process. It guides you through identifying your learning style, setting achievable goals, and managing your time effectively. The idea is to make learning a more streamlined and less overwhelming process.

This guide takes a holistic approach to learning. It explores how factors like memory, critical thinking, and even your physical and mental health significantly influence how well and quickly you learn. It also highlights the importance of technology and digital tools in today's learning landscape, showing you how to use these resources effectively.

In essence, "How to Learn Almost Anything in 48 Hours" isn't just about learning fast and well? It provides a practical framework that can be applied to any subject or skill, transforming how you approach learning. The book is more than a collection of strategies; it is an invitation to change your mind set about learning, showing you that rapid learning is within your reach with the right approach.

## Debunking myths about learning capacities and time constraints

In tackling the myths about learning capacities and time constraints, it's essential to understand that learning quickly and effectively is not just for a select few with exceptional talents. Many people believe that you either have a natural ability to learn rapidly or you don't and that learning anything substantial requires a lot of time. However, this is only sometimes true.

Everyone has the potential to learn new skills or information quickly. It's not about being born with a specific 'learning gene' but using the proper techniques and approaches. The key is in how you approach the learning process. By adopting effective strategies, such as breaking down complex information into smaller, manageable parts or using memory aids, you can significantly speed up your learning.

Also, the idea that learning always takes a long time is another myth that needs rethinking. While some skills and subjects can be complex and require more time to master, many can be learned in a shorter period of time than traditionally thought. It's about being efficient in your learning process, focusing on key concepts, and practicing to reinforce what you've learned quickly.

So, debunking these myths is all about understanding that rapid learning is accessible to everyone and that the time it takes to learn something new can often be shorter than you think with the right approach and techniques.

## Success stories of rapid learning

Talking about rapid learning, there are some fantastic stories out there that show just how effective it can be. Take the story of a young woman who wanted to switch her career to web development. She only had a little background in coding, but she was determined. Within just a couple of months, she could build her website from scratch by focusing intensely on online courses and practicing every day. Her dedication paid off when she landed a job as a junior developer, something she thought would take at least a year to achieve.

Then there's the example of a man in his thirties who decided to learn Spanish for his upcoming trip to South America. He had only six weeks before his trip. Most people would think that's not enough time to learn a new language, but he used various methods like language apps, speaking with native speakers online, and immersing himself in Spanish music and films. When he flew out, he could converse with locals, making his travel experience more prosperous. These stories are just a couple of examples of how rapid learning can lead to actual, tangible results with the right approach and dedication. It's about putting in the hours and being smart with your time and resources. Whether changing careers, picking up a new language, or learning a new skill, the possibilities are endless when you know how to learn effectively and quickly.

# CHAPTER 2

# UNDERSTANDING YOUR LEARNING STYLE

When discussing learning styles, we dive into how people grasp and understand new information. Everyone has a unique approach to learning; understanding these can make a huge difference in how effectively we learn. Let's look at the most common learning styles: visual, auditory, and kinesthetic.

As the name suggests, visual learners learn best when they have images or visual aids to help them understand the information. These learners thrive on diagrams, charts, and anything they can see. For example, suppose a visual learner is trying to understand a complex concept. In that case, a well-organized chart or a vibrant info graphic can be more helpful than listening to a lecture or reading a text. They remember things better when they see them. If you're a visual learner, you might find yourself drawn to books with lots of pictures, or you might be someone who benefits from making concept maps or visual notes when studying.

Then there are auditory learners. These learners prefer to hear information rather than read it or see it visually. They learn best through listening to lectures, discussions, or audio recordings. For an auditory learner, reading from a textbook might be less effective than attending a class or participating in a group discussion. They often benefit from reading out loud or having someone else read to them. If you're an auditory learner, you remember things better when you talk them through or listen to podcasts or audio books.

Kinesthetic learners are all about touch and movement. They learn best by doing. These learners need to engage with the material to understand it physically. They prefer hands-on experiences, experiments, and real-life examples over theoretical or abstract learning. For a kinesthetic learner, sitting still and listening to a lecture or reading a book might not cut it. They benefit from building models, performing experiments, or even moving around while studying. If you're a kinesthetic learner, remember things better when you can physically engage with the subject matter, like role-playing or building something related to your learning.

Apart from these three, other learning styles, like reading/writing-preferred learners, learn best by reading texts and writing notes. Some people combine different types and must fit more neatly into one category. They might be a mix of visual and auditory or kinesthetic and reading/writing. It's also important to note that learning styles can evolve and differ depending on the subject matter.

Understanding your learning style is crucial because it can help you study more effectively. Imagine you're a visual learner stuck in a class that's all lectures and no visuals. You might find it hard to grasp the material, not because it's difficult, but because it's not being presented in a way that aligns with how you learn best. By knowing your learning style, you can adapt your study methods. For instance, if you're an auditory learner in a heavily visual class, you might benefit from recording the lectures and listening to them later.

Learning styles play a significant role in how we absorb and process information. Whether you're a visual, auditory, kinesthetic, or reading/writing learner, understanding your style can help you tailor your learning process more effectively. It's about making the learning journey as smooth and efficient as possible in a way that resonates with your natural preferences. So, take a moment to think about how you prefer to learn. It is the key to unlocking your learning potential.

## Self-assessment to determine your learning style

Figuring out your learning style is like unlocking a secret code that makes learning more accessible and practical. It's all about understanding how you process and retain information best. While many formal assessments and quizzes can help you determine your learning style, you can also do a simple self-assessment by observing how you naturally tend to learn and remember things.

Start by reflecting on your past learning experiences. Think about a time when you learned something well. What was happening? Were you listening to someone explain it, watching a demonstration, doing the activity yourself, or reading and writing about it? Your best learning experiences can give you a clue about your preferred learning style.

You might be a visual learner if you find that you remember things better when you see them, like through diagrams, charts, or even when you visualize them in your mind. Visual learners often remember faces better than names, prefer reading over listening and use color coding in their notes. They usually do well with maps and can often recall information by remembering where it was on a page or a slide.

On the other hand, if you remember things better when you hear them, like in a lecture or a podcast, or prefer to talk through a problem or a concept to understand it better, you're likely an auditory learner. Auditory learners often remember what they hear very clearly, like the tone of someone's voice or the details of a story. They might prefer oral exams to written ones and enjoy group discussions or debates.

If you can't sit still for long, like to tinker with things and find you understand something better when you can use your hands or move around, you might be a kinesthetic learner. Kinesthetic learners often do well in labs, enjoy field trips, and remember what was done rather than what was said or seen. They usually have difficulty sitting through lectures without fidgeting and may learn better when taking frequent breaks to move around.

Some people find that they need to fit more neatly into one category but are a mix of different styles. You might be predominantly a visual learner but find auditory techniques helpful in certain situations. Or you might be a kinesthetic learner who also benefits from writing things down. That's completely normal. Most people use a mix of learning styles depending on the subject or context.

Once you have an idea of your learning style, try integrating it into your study or learning new things. If you're a visual learner, use images, charts, and diagrams to help you understand and remember information. If you're an auditory learner, try to attend lectures or discussions or use audio books and podcasts as learning tools. If you're a kinesthetic learner, look for opportunities to learn through hands-on experiences, whether building models, doing experiments, or just moving around while studying.

Remember, knowing your learning style isn't about limiting yourself to one way of learning. It's about understanding your natural preferences so you can tailor your learning strategies to be more effective. It's perfectly okay to use different styles for different types of learning and to explore new ways of learning that might not be your preferred style. The goal is to make your learning experience as effective and enjoyable as possible.

## Tailoring learning methods to fit your style

When it comes to learning, one size doesn't fit all. That's why tailoring your learning methods to fit your style is essential. Once you understand whether you're a visual, auditory, kinesthetic, or mixed-style learner, you can start to adapt the way you study and learn to suit your needs. This can significantly affect how quickly and effectively you absorb information.

You've figured out that you're a visual learner. You learn best with images, diagrams, and visual aids to help you understand information. How can you apply this to your learning? Start by incorporating more visuals into your study materials. Use charts, graphs, and info graphics whenever you can. When you take notes, try to use visual organizers like mind maps or concept maps. These tools can help you see the connections between ideas and make the information more memorable. Try creating your own if you're studying something that doesn't naturally lend itself to visuals. Draw diagrams or sketches that help you understand the concepts. Even making the visual aid can help reinforce what you're learning.

If you're an auditory learner, you'll focus on using sound, rhythm, and music to help you learn. You remember information better if you hear it spoken, so try to attend lectures or participate in group discussions whenever possible. When studying independently, you can read your notes out loud or explain the material to someone else. Recording yourself speaking the material and listening to it can also be helpful. Additionally, use auditory resources like audio books, podcasts, or educational videos. Setting information to music or a rhythm helps you remember it more effectively.

For kinesthetic learners, the key is to get active with your learning. Since you learn best when moving around and using your hands, try incorporating physical activities into your study routine. This could be as simple as walking around while you review your notes or as involved as doing a hands-on project or experiment. If you're studying something abstract, try to find a way to create a physical representation of it, like a model or a role-play. Even just using flashcards can be helpful since it involves a physical action. Taking frequent, short breaks for movement can help you stay focused and retain information better.

If you're a mixed-style learner, you have the advantage of flexibility. You can mix and match different strategies to find what works best for you in different situations. Maybe you use visual aids for one subject, but find that discussion and audio resources work better for another. The key is to be willing to experiment and adjust your strategies as needed.

No matter what your learning style, there are a few general strategies that can help. First, try to stay organized. Keeping your study materials well-organized can make focusing and understanding the material more accessible. This might mean different things depending on your learning style. For a visual learner, it might mean color-coding notes and materials. For an auditory learner, it might mean having neatly organized audio files.

Second, try to make your learning active rather than passive. Instead of just reading or listening to the material, try to engage with it. This could mean discussing it, teaching it to someone else, or applying it to a real-world problem. Active learning helps to reinforce the material and make it more memorable.

# CHAPTER 3

# SETTING CLEAR GOALS AND OBJECTIVES

Understanding the importance of setting goals in the learning process is crucial for anyone who wants to enhance their learning experience. Goal-setting is about creating targets and providing direction and motivation, making the learning journey more focused and efficient. Whether you're a student tackling a new subject, a professional learning a new skill or just someone who enjoys learning new things, this concept is essential.

The first benefit of setting goals is giving you a clear direction. When you select a goal, you decide where you want to go. This is especially helpful when you're learning something new or complex. Without a clear plan, it's easy to feel overwhelmed or lose track of what you're trying to achieve. But when you have a goal, you have a roadmap to follow. It helps you focus on what's important and avoid getting sidetracked by things that don't need to be more relevant to your ultimate objective.

Another advantage of setting goals is that it helps you measure your progress. This is incredibly motivating. When you have a plan, you can see how far you've come and how much closer you are to achieving it. This can be a huge motivator, especially when learning something challenging. It's satisfying to see your progress, and it can encourage you to keep going, even when things get tough.

Goals also help you stay committed. Learning something new requires time, effort, and sometimes even a bit of struggle. When you're facing a complex topic or a skill that's hard to master, it's easy to feel like giving up. But you have a reason to keep going if you have a clear goal. Your goal reminds you of why you're learning in the first place and what you hope to achieve. This can be a powerful motivator to stick with your learning, even when challenging.

Setting goals also makes your learning more efficient. When you have a dream, you can plan your knowledge more effectively. You can decide what resources you need, what strategies to use, and how much time to devote to different aspects of your understanding. This planning can make your learning process much more efficient. Instead of wasting time on things that aren't helpful, you can focus your efforts on what will help you achieve your goal.

Goals can also help you overcome obstacles. You're more likely to find ways to overcome challenges and keep moving forward when working towards a goal. If you encounter a complex topic or a skill that's hard to master, having a plan can motivate you to find resources, seek help, or try different strategies until you overcome the obstacle.

Finally, goal-setting can make learning more enjoyable. When you have a goal, you're working towards something meaningful. This can make the learning process feel more rewarding and enjoyable. Instead of just going through the motions, you're actively working towards something you care about. This can make the learning experience much more satisfying.

In conclusion, setting goals is a vital part of the learning process. It provides direction, motivation, and a way to measure progress. It helps you stay committed, makes your learning more efficient, enables you to overcome obstacles, and can make learning more enjoyable. Whether you're learning something for school, work, or fun, setting clear goals can help you achieve more and enjoy the process more. So, next time you start a new learning project, take some time to set some clear, achievable goals. It is the key to your success.

## How to define clear, achievable learning objectives

Defining clear and achievable learning objectives is vital in the learning process. It's like setting the destination before starting a journey. These objectives guide you through your learning, giving you a clear idea of what you must achieve and helping you stay on track. But how do you set these objectives to be clear and achievable?

The first step is to be specific about what you want to learn. Vague goals like "I want to learn Spanish" or "I want to get better at math" are too broad and don't give you a clear target. Instead, break these down into more specific objectives. For example, "I want to learn how to introduce myself and have a basic conversation in Spanish" or "I want to understand and solve algebraic equations." These are more specific and give you a clear idea of what you need to focus on.

Once you have a specific objective, make sure it's measurable. This means setting a goal that you can assess whether you've achieved it or not. For instance, rather than saying, "I want to be good at coding," say, "I want to be able to write a simple program using Python." It's easier to measure your success with the latter because you can complete a specific task to show you've met your objective.

It's also essential that your objectives are achievable. This doesn't mean setting easy goals but rather realistic goals for your current level and circumstances. If you're starting to learn a language, setting a goal to be fluent in three months might not be realistic. However, aiming to learn basic phrases and conversational skills in that time might be more doable.

Your objectives should also be relevant to your overall learning goals. If you're learning a language to travel, your dreams should focus on conversational skills and understanding culture rather than deep grammar rules. If you're learning a new skill for work, focus on the aspects of that skill that will be most useful in your job.

Set a time frame for your objectives. Without a deadline, it's easy to keep putting off your learning. Decide when you want to achieve your goals, and then work backward to create a timeline. This helps you to stay focused and motivated.

The process of setting objectives isn't static. Your goals might change as you progress in your learning, and that's okay. It's essential to review and adjust your objectives as needed. This might mean making them more challenging as you improve or changing them if you realize they must help you achieve your learning goals.

Setting clear and achievable learning objectives involves:

- Being specific.
- Making sure they are measurable.
- Ensuring they are achievable and realistic.
- Keeping them relevant
- Setting a time frame.

By following these guidelines, you can create objectives that guide your learning effectively, helping you to focus your efforts and see real progress in your learning journey.

## Techniques for maintaining focus and motivation

Maintaining focus and motivation while learning can sometimes feel like a challenge. We've all been there, trying to learn something new or work on a project and then finding ourselves distracted or losing interest. However, some practical techniques can help you stay focused and keep your motivation high.

One essential technique is to set small, manageable goals. Staying motivated can be overwhelming and complicated when you have a big plan. But breaking it down into smaller, more manageable parts can make it feel more achievable and less daunting. For example, if you're trying to learn a new language, instead of setting a goal to be fluent, start with smaller goals like learning ten new words daily. Achieving these smaller goals can give you a sense of accomplishment and motivate you to continue.

Another essential technique is to create a regular study schedule. Our brains like routine and having a set time each day for studying can help keep you on track. Try to find a time of day when you're alert and focused, and make that your regular study time. This will help you develop a studying habit and make it easier to focus.

It's also helpful to minimize distractions. This might mean finding a quiet place to study, turning off notifications on your phone, or using apps that block distracting websites. Everyone's distractions are different, so determine what tends to distract your attention from studying and find ways to minimize those distractions.

Another technique is to vary your study methods. Doing the same thing over and over can get boring and make it hard to stay motivated. Try mixing up your study methods to keep things interesting. If you usually read textbooks, try watching a video or doing a hands-on project. If you're studying a language, mix up vocabulary drills with conversations or watching movies in the language. Changing things can keep your brain engaged and make learning more enjoyable.

Rewarding yourself can also be a great motivator. Set up a reward system for yourself for meeting your study goals. This could be something minor, like treating yourself to your favorite snack after a study session, or something bigger, like going out with friends after you finish a big project. Having something to look forward to can help you stay motivated to reach your goals.

It's also essential to take regular breaks. Studying for long periods without a break can lead to burnout and make focusing hard. Try using techniques like the Commodore Technique, where you look for 25 minutes and then take a 5-minute break. This can help you stay focused during your study time and allow your brain to rest and recharge.

Staying physically active can also help with focus and motivation. Exercise can increase blood flow to the brain and help you feel more alert and focused. It doesn't have to be intense exercise; even a short walk or stretching can help.

Stay positive and be kind to yourself. Having off days is normal when you're less focused or motivated. Don't be too hard on yourself when this happens. Remind yourself of why you're learning and what you're working towards. Celebrating your progress, no matter how small, can also help keep you motivated.

Maintaining focus and motivation involves:

- Setting small goals.
- Creating a regular study schedule.
- Minimizing distractions.
- Varying your study methods
- Rewarding you.
- Taking regular breaks.
- Staying physically active.
- Staying positive.

Using these techniques lets you keep yourself focused and motivated throughout your learning journey.

# CHAPTER 4

## TIME MANAGEMENT FOR EFFECTIVE LEARNING

Managing your time efficiently is crucial, especially when trying to learn something new or juggling multiple responsibilities. It's easy to feel like there need to be more hours in the day, but you can make the most of your time with the right strategies. Here are some techniques to help you manage your time more effectively.

First, it's essential to prioritize your tasks. Not all jobs are equal; some are more important or urgent than others. By figuring out which tasks are the most important, you can focus your time and energy where needed most. One way to do this is to make a to-do list and rank each task based on importance and urgency. Focus on the tasks at the top of your list first and work your way down. This helps ensure that you're always working on what's most important.

Another critical strategy is to plan your time. This means setting aside specific times for specific tasks. For example, you might study every day from 6 pm to 8 pm. Having a plan helps you stay organized and focused, preventing you from wasting time deciding what to do next. When planning your time, be realistic about how long tasks will take and build in extra time for unexpected delays or interruptions.

Breaking big tasks into smaller, more manageable parts helps with time management. Large tasks can be overwhelming and hard to start, but smaller jobs feel more doable. For example, if you have a big project, break it down into smaller steps like researching, writing an outline, and writing each section. This makes it easier to start and helps you keep track of your progress.

Setting deadlines can also be a helpful way to manage your time. Deadlines create a sense of urgency and can help motivate you to finish tasks. When setting deadlines, be realistic and give yourself enough time to complete the job without rushing. It's also helpful to set reminders for your deadlines so you remember them.

Avoiding multitasking is another critical time management strategy. While it might seem like you're getting more done by doing multiple things simultaneously, it can be less efficient. Multitasking can make it harder to focus and lower the quality of your work. Instead, try to focus on one task at a time and give it your full attention. This can help you work more efficiently and produce better results.

Another technique is to use your time wisely. This means finding ways to make the most of the time you have. For example, if you have a long commute, you could use that time to listen to an educational podcast or audio book. Or, if you find that you're more alert and focused in the morning, try to schedule your most important tasks for that time.

It's also essential to eliminate or minimize distractions. Distractions can save time and make focusing on what you must do easier. Identify what your biggest distractions are and find ways to reduce them. This might mean turning off your phone notifications, finding a quiet workplace, or using apps blocking distracting websites.

It might seem counterintuitive, but regular intervals can help you manage your time better. Holidays give your brain a chance to rest and recharge, which can help you stay focused and productive when you're working. Just ensure your holidays are short and don't become long distractions.

Effective time management involves prioritizing tasks, planning your time, breaking down big tasks, setting deadlines, avoiding multitasking, using your time wisely, minimizing distractions, and taking breaks. Using these strategies lets you make the most of your time and get more done.

## Balancing learning with other life responsibilities

Balancing learning with other life responsibilities can be a tough act. Whether you're a student, a working professional, or someone trying to pick up a new skill or hobby, finding the right balance between studying and the rest of your life is crucial. It ensures your learning balances your work, family time, social energy, and well-being.

The key to finding this balance understands that effective learning isn't about cramming in as much study time as possible. It's about studying smart. This means being strategic about how and when you learn so it fits seamlessly with the rest of your life. The first step in achieving this is setting realistic goals. Consider all your other responsibilities, and be honest about how much time you can dedicate to learning. Overloading yourself with unrealistic study goals can lead to burnout and stress, making learning less effective.

Creating a schedule can help a lot. When you have a clear plan for when you're going to study, it's easier to manage your time and ensure that you're giving enough attention to other areas of your life. Identify times in your day when you're usually free and can focus without interruptions. This could be early in the morning before work, during lunch breaks, or in the evening. Consistency is key here. If you can study simultaneously every day, it becomes part of your routine, just like eating or sleeping.

Another important aspect is learning to prioritize and say no. Life is full of demands and distractions, and it's easy to over commit yourself. Learn to prioritize tasks and responsibilities that align with your goals and values. Sometimes, this might mean saying no to social events or extra projects to give you enough time for learning and other vital tasks. Remember, it's about quality, not quantity.

It's also vital to make use of efficient learning strategies. This means finding ways to learn that get you the best results in the least amount of time. For example, if you're a visual learner, using charts and diagrams can help you understand concepts faster than just reading text. Listening to lectures or podcasts might be more effective if you're an auditory learner. Using the right strategies can help you learn more in less time, freeing up time for other activities.

Remember to integrate learning into your daily life. Sometimes, you can combine learning with other activities. For example, if you're learning a new language, you can listen to language lessons or audio books while commuting or doing chores. Or, if you're learning to cook, you can experiment with new recipes for your family's dinner. This way, learning doesn't feel like a separate, time-consuming task but becomes a part of your everyday life.

It's also essential to take breaks and give yourself time to relax. Continuous learning without breaks can lead to exhaustion and make it hard to retain information. Take short breaks during study sessions and set aside time for relaxation and leisure activities. This helps prevent burnout and improves overall productivity and learning efficiency.

Balancing learning with other life responsibilities also means being kind to you. There will be days when life gets in the way, and you might be unable to stick to your study schedule. That's okay. Be flexible and adjust your plan as needed. You keep a long-term perspective and remember that occasional setbacks won't derail your overall progress.

Balancing learning with other life responsibilities requires realistic goal-setting, effective time management, prioritization, and efficient learning strategies, integrating learning into your daily life, taking breaks, and being kind to yourself. By adopting these approaches, you can make learning a fulfilling part of your life without compromising your work, family time, or personal well-being.

## Overcoming procrastination and distractions

Overcoming procrastination and distractions is a common challenge, especially in a world filled with constant notifications and endless to-do lists. Whether studying for a big exam, working on a project, or trying to learn something new, staying focused and avoiding procrastination can sometimes feel like a battle. But with some practical strategies, you can overcome these hurdles and maintain a steady pace in your work or learning.

The first step in overcoming procrastination understands why it happens. We often need to work on time because a task seems too big, complex, or tedious. It feels easier to put it off than to face it. The trick is to break down these giant, intimidating tasks into smaller, more manageable pieces. For example, if you need more time to start a big project, break it down into smaller steps like outlining, researching, and writing sections. This makes the task seem less daunting and more doable.

Setting small, achievable goals can also help. Instead of aiming to complete the entire project in one go, set a goal to finish just the first part.

Small goals are less intimidating, and completing them gives you a sense of accomplishment that can motivate you to keep going. Each small step completed is progress, and it helps build momentum.

Another effective strategy is to change your environment. Sometimes, our usual study or work environment is filled with distractions that make procrastination easier. Changing your surroundings can help reset your focus. This could be as simple as cleaning up your workspace to remove clutter or moving to a different location like a library or a quiet cafe. A change in environment can break the cycle of procrastination and give you a fresh perspective.

Limiting distractions is crucial. In today's digital world, smart phones, social media, and email can be significant distractions. One way to deal with this is to set specific times for checking emails or social media and stick to it. Consider using apps that block distracting websites or turning off notifications on your phone during work or study time. The fewer distractions tempt you, the easier it is to stay focused.

Timers can be a great tool against procrastination. Techniques like the Commodore Technique, where you work for 25 minutes and then take a 5-minute break, can be very effective. This method helps you stay focused for short bursts, making the task feel less overwhelming. The short breaks also provide a quick rest for your brain, keeping you fresh and preventing burnout.

It's also important to understand your productive times. Everyone has times of the day when they feel more alert and focused. For some, it's in the morning; for others, it's late at night. Find out when you're most productive and try to schedule your most challenging tasks for these times. Working when you're at your best can help you get more done and reduce the temptation to procrastinate.

Self-compassion is essential to overcoming procrastination. Beating yourself up for procrastinating only adds to the stress and makes starting harder. Instead, acknowledge procrastination is a common challenge and be kind to yourself. When you notice you're procrastinating, gently guide yourself back to the task without judgment.

Lastly, understand that overcoming procrastination is a process. It's not something that will change overnight. It requires practice and patience. Celebrate the small victories, like a productive work session or a day without falling into procrastination traps. Over time, these small successes add up, and you'll find yourself procrastinating less and less.

Overcoming procrastination and distractions involves:

- Breaking tasks into smaller parts.
- Setting achievable goals.
- Changing your environment.
- Limiting distractions.
- Using timers.
- Working during your productive times.
- Practicing self-compassion.
- Be patient with yourself.

Adopting these strategies can reduce procrastination and stay focused on your tasks, leading to better productivity and a more rewarding learning or working experience.

# CHAPTER 5

## MEMORY ENHANCEMENT TECHNIQUES

Understanding memory is fascinating and essential, especially when learning and retaining information. Our memory is like a vast and complex storage system that helps us recall past experiences, learn new information, and perform tasks. But how does it work?

Memory involves three fundamental processes: encoding, storage, and retrieval. Encoding is the first step. It's like entering data into a computer. When you learn something new, your brain encodes the information into a form that can be stored. This process involves paying attention to the information and linking it to things you already know or your experiences. For example, when you meet someone new, your brain encodes their name by connecting it to their face and perhaps other details like where you met them or what they do.

Storage is the second step. This is where the encoded information is kept in your brain. There are different types of memory storage, each playing a different role. Short-term memory holds information briefly, like remembering a phone number long enough to dial it. Long-term memory, on the other hand, is for information that you retain for a more extended period, from a few days to decades. This includes things like your language knowledge, childhood memories, or skills like riding a bike.

The third step is retrieval when you recall or use stored information. This can happen automatically, like remembering how to drive when you get in a car or requiring more effort, like identifying information for a test. The ease with which you can retrieve information depends on several factors, including how the data was encoded and how often it's been recalled.

One interesting thing about memory is that it's not static. Every time you recall a memory, it can change slightly. This is because recalling a memory involves reconstructing it, and during this process, new details can be added, or some elements can be forgotten. That's why people's recollections of the same event can differ.

Our ability to remember things can also be affected by various factors. For example, stress, lack of sleep, and poor nutrition can all make it harder to focus and encode new information. On the other hand, things like regular exercise, a healthy diet, and sufficient sleep can enhance memory function.

Another important aspect of memory is the role of repetition and practice. When you repeatedly go over information, it strengthens the neural connections in your brain, making it easier to recall the information later. This is why studying over some time is usually more effective than cramming all the information in one night.

Memory can also be enhanced through mnemonics, which involves creating associations or patterns to help remember information. For example, using a rhyme or an acronym can make remembering a list of items or a complex concept easier.

Understanding how memory works can significantly improve how you learn and retain information. By paying attention to how you encode information, storing it effectively through practice and repetition, and using techniques to aid retrieval, you can enhance your memory and make your learning more effective.

Memory involves encoding, storing, and retrieving information. It is influenced by how we pay attention, link new information to what we already know, and our overall health and well-being. By understanding how memory works and using strategies to support it, you can improve your ability to remember and use information, a vital part of learning and navigating everyday life.

## Techniques to improve memory retention

Improving memory retention is essential for effective learning and can significantly affect how well you remember information. You can use several techniques to boost your memory, including mnemonics, visualization, and more.

Mnemonics are one of the most popular memory aids. They create a simple way to remember a list of items or concepts. A common mnemonic technique is to use acronyms, where you take the first letter of each thing you need to remember and create a word or phrase out of those letters. For example, many people remember the rainbow colors (Red, Orange, Yellow, Green, Blue, Indigo, and Violet) using the acronym ROYGBIV. Another mnemonic technique is to create a rhyme or a song, as rhyming words and melodies can be easier to remember than plain text.

Visualization is another powerful memory technique. This involves creating a mental image of what you're trying to remember. For instance, if you're trying to remember a grocery list, you might visualize walking through the grocery store and picking up each item. Visualization works because it better fits the brain's natural ability to remember images and spatial information than abstract data.

Another effective memory technique is the method of loci, also known as the memory palace. This method involves visualizing a familiar place, like your home or a path you walk often, and placing the items you need to remember at different locations in that space. For example, if you're trying to remember a list of historical dates, you might visualize the first date at your front door, the second date on the living room couch, and so on. When you need to recall the information, you mentally walk through your memory palace, and the locations help trigger your memory of each item.

Repetition also plays a crucial role in memory retention. Going over information repeatedly helps to reinforce it in your mind. This could be as simple as rereading your notes several times or practicing a skill regularly. Spaced repetition is particularly effective when you review information at increasing intervals over time. For example, you might check your notes one day after you learn something, three days later, a week later, and so on. This technique works because it helps prevent natural forgetting over time.

Teaching the information to someone else is a great way to improve memory retention. When you teach, you have to organize the news in your own words, which helps to reinforce it in your memory. It also forces you to recall the information more actively than rereading it.

Connecting new information to things you already know is another effective memory technique. When you can relate further information to existing knowledge, it helps to anchor it in your mind. For example, if you're learning about a new scientific concept, thinking about how it relates to something you already understand can make remembering easier.

Taking care of your overall health can also improve memory retention. Getting enough sleep, eating a healthy diet, staying hydrated, and exercising regularly all contribute to better brain function, which includes memory. Stress reduction techniques like meditation or deep breathing can also help, as stress can negatively impact memory.

You can use many techniques to improve memory retention, including mnemonics, visualization, the method of loci, repetition, teaching others, connecting new information to what you already know, and taking care of your overall health. Incorporating these techniques into your study habits can enhance your ability to remember and recall information, making your learning more effective and efficient.

## Practice exercises for memory enhancement

Practicing exercises for memory enhancement is a great way to keep your brain sharp and improve your ability to remember things. Like any other skill, memory can be enhanced with the right exercises and techniques. These exercises don't have to be complicated; many are simple and can be incorporated into your daily routine.

One of the most effective exercises for memory enhancement is practicing recall. After learning something new, take a break and try to recall the information without looking at your notes. This could be right after a class or a study session. Try to remember as much as you can about what you just learned. You can do this aloud, write it down, or even draw it, depending on what works best for you. This exercise helps reinforce the information in your memory and makes it easier to recall later.

Another great exercise is regularly challenging your brain with puzzles and games that require memory. This includes crossword puzzles, Sudoku, memory card games, or even Smartphone apps designed to improve memory. These games keep your brain active and can improve both short-term and long-term memory skills. Plus, they're fun to do, which makes the exercise seem less like work and more like play.

Learning something new every day is another way to enhance memory. This could be anything from a new word in a foreign language to a fact about history or science. Learning further information regularly keeps your brain engaged and improves memory retention. You can set a goal for yourself, like learning a new word each day, and make it a part of your daily routine.

Teaching others what you've learned is also a great memory exercise. When you teach information to someone else, you must remember it well enough to explain it clearly. This forces you to retrieve the data from memory, strengthening your recall. It can be as simple as telling a friend about a new concept you learned in a class or teaching a family member how to do something.

Regular physical exercise is also beneficial for memory. Physical activities, especially aerobic exercises like walking, running, swimming, or cycling, increase blood flow to the entire body, including the brain. This can help improve cognitive functions, including memory. Even a short walk each day can make a difference.

Meditation and mindfulness exercises can also enhance memory. These practices help reduce stress, which can negatively affect memory. They also improve concentration and focus, making it easier to encode new information and recall it later. You can start with just a few minutes of meditation or mindfulness each day and gradually increase the time.

Finally, getting enough sleep is essential for memory enhancement. Sleep is critical in memory consolidation, forming and storing new memories. Ensuring you get enough quality sleep each night can significantly improve your ability to remember information.

Exercises for memory enhancement include:

- Practicing recall.
- Playing memory-boosting games and puzzles.
- Learning something new every day.
- Teaching others.
- Engaging in regular physical activity.
- Practicing meditation and mindfulness.
- Getting enough sleep.

These exercises are simple to incorporate into daily life and can significantly improve memory. Regularly practicing these exercises can keep your brain sharp and improve your ability to remember and recall information.

# CHAPTER 6

# CRITICAL THINKING AND UNDERSTANDING

Developing critical thinking skills is vital to learning and can benefit almost every aspect of life. Critical thinking involves analyzing and evaluating information to form a reasoned judgment. It's about being an active learner rather than a passive recipient of information. This skill can be learned and improved with practice, and there are several ways to develop your critical thinking skills.

One of the first steps in developing critical thinking is to ask questions. Don't just take information at face value. Ask yourself what the information means, how it fits into the bigger picture, and whether it's reliable. For example, when reading a news article, consider the source, the evidence provided, and the potential biases. Asking questions helps you dig deeper into the information and understand it more fully.

Another important aspect of critical thinking is to be open-minded. This means being willing to consider different perspectives and viewpoints. When you're open to other ways of looking at things, it challenges your beliefs and assumptions and can lead to a deeper understanding. Try to listen to and understand different viewpoints, even if you don't agree with them. This can be a challenging but rewarding part of developing critical thinking skills.

Analyzing arguments is also a key part of critical thinking. This involves looking at the structure of an argument and evaluating its validity. When you hear or read an argument, think about the evidence being presented and whether it logically supports the conclusion. Look for any flaws in the reasoning or gaps in the evidence. This will help you to determine whether the argument is sound or not.

Another technique for developing critical thinking is to practice problem-solving. This involves identifying a problem, gathering information, evaluating options, and deciding. This process requires critical thinking to weigh the options and decide on the best action. Problem-solving can be practiced in many areas of life, from small everyday problems to larger, more complex issues.

Reflecting on your beliefs and values is also important to critical thinking. Sometimes, our beliefs and values can influence our thinking without realizing it. By reflecting on these, you can become more aware of how they might affect your judgment. This self-awareness can help you to think more objectively and critically.

Discussing ideas with others can also help develop your critical thinking skills. Conversations and debates with other people can expose you to different viewpoints and help you to refine your arguments. When discussing ideas, listen actively and understand the other person's point of view, even if you disagree. This can help you to develop a more rounded and informed perspective.

Practice is key to developing critical thinking skills. Like any skill, the more you practice, the better you get. Try to incorporate critical thinking into your daily life. Whenever you're presented with information, take a moment to think about it critically. Ask questions, analyze arguments, and consider different perspectives. The more you practice, the more natural it will become.

Developing critical thinking skills involves:

- Asking questions.
- Being open-minded.
- Analyzing arguments.
- Practicing problem-solving.
- Reflecting on your beliefs and values.
- Discussing ideas with others.
- Practicing regularly.

These skills are not only important for academic success but are also valuable in everyday life. You can become a more informed and effective thinker by developing your critical thinking skills.

## Techniques for deeper understanding of material

A deeper understanding of the material is a goal for anyone who wants to learn and truly grasp and master a subject. This deep understanding enables you to apply knowledge in new ways, see connections between ideas, and think critically about what you've learned. Several techniques over beyond surface-level learning to get to of the material.

One effective technique is active learning. This means engaging with the material dynamically rather than just passively reading or listening. Active learning could involve:

- Discussing the material with others.
- Teaching it to someone else.
- Applying it in a practical project.
- Even asking yourself questions about your learning.

For example, if you're studying a historical event, instead of just reading about it, you could debate its causes and effects with classmates or write a diary entry from the perspective of someone who lived through it. These activities require you to process the information more deeply, helping to cement your understanding.

Another key technique is to connect what you're learning and what you already know. This can involve relating new concepts to your own experiences, other things you've learned, or real-world examples. Making these connections helps to anchor the new information in your memory and gives it more meaning. For instance, if you're learning a new scientific concept, thinking about how it relates to everyday phenomena can make it more understandable and memorable.

Critical thinking is also important for deepening your understanding. This means not just taking in information but analyzing it, questioning it, and considering it from different perspectives. When you practice critical thinking, you're not just learning what something is; you understand why it's that way, how it fits into a broader context, and what implications it has. This thinking can be developed by asking probing questions, looking for evidence, and evaluating different viewpoints.

Concept mapping is another useful tool. This involves creating a visual diagram that shows the relationships between different concepts. By mapping out the material, you can see how the pieces fit together, which can help you, understand the bigger picture. This is particularly helpful for complex subjects with lots of interconnected parts.

Another technique is to regularly review and reflect on what you've learned. This doesn't just mean rereading your notes or textbooks. It means thinking about what the material means, how it applies to different situations, and what questions it raises. Reflecting in this way helps to consolidate your understanding and allows you to process the information more deeply.

Teaching the material to someone else is also a powerful way to deepen your understanding. When you teach, you have to explain the concepts clearly and answer questions, which force you to think about the material in a new way and understand it more fully. Even if you don't have an actual audience, you can practice this technique by imagining you teaching the material or explaining it to a friend or family member.

Lastly, practice and application are crucial. The more you use the information, the better you'll understand it. This could involve solving problems, doing practical projects, or applying the concepts in real-life situations. Using the information reinforces your understanding and helps you see how it can be applied in different contexts.

Techniques for a deeper understanding of the material include:

- Active learning.
- Making connections.
- Practicing critical thinking.
- Using concept mapping.
- Reflecting on what you've learned.
- Teaching others.
- Practicing and applying the concepts.

These techniques require more effort than just reading or memorizing, but they lead to a much richer and more meaningful understanding of the material. Using these techniques, you can move beyond just knowing facts to understanding and using what you've learned.

## Applying knowledge in practical scenarios

Applying knowledge in practical scenarios is a crucial step in the learning process. It's one thing to understand a concept in theory but another to use that knowledge in real-world situations. This application reinforces your learning and enhances your problem-solving skills and ability to adapt knowledge to different contexts.

One of the first steps in applying knowledge is recognizing the real-world relevance of your learning. For every concept or skill you learn, consider where and how it could be used in everyday life. For instance, if you're learning about budgeting in a finance class, try applying those principles to manage your finances. Or, if you're learning a new language, use it to converse with native speakers or watch movies in that language. Seeing the practical application of your learning makes the material more interesting and memorable.

Another key aspect of applying knowledge is to engage in hands-on projects or activities. Depending on your learning, this could be anything from a science experiment to a programming project. These activities allow you to use your knowledge in a practical setting, which can deepen your understanding and reveal areas where you need more practice or study.

Working on real-life problems is also a great way to apply your knowledge. This could involve participating in competitions, working on community projects, or even helping solve everyday problems. When you apply what you've learned to solve real problems, it not only reinforces your knowledge but also improves your critical thinking and creativity.

Seeking internships or work experiences related to your field of study is another way to apply your knowledge. This experience is invaluable because it puts you in real-world situations where you must use what you've learned. It also gives you a taste of what working in that field might be like, which can be incredibly helpful in choosing a career path.

Teaching others what you've learned is also an effective way to apply your knowledge. When you teach, you have to think about the material in a way that makes it clear and understandable to someone else. This process can deepen your understanding and reveal gaps in your knowledge. Plus, it's a great way to reinforce what you've learned.

Another technique is regularly reflecting on your learning and considering how it applies to different scenarios. This could involve writing about what you've learned, discussing it with friends or classmates, or even thinking about it in your free time. Reflecting in this way helps you connect the material and real-world situations.

Don't be afraid to experiment and make mistakes. Applying knowledge often involves trial and error, especially when trying something new. Mistakes are a natural part of the learning process and can be valuable. They show you what doesn't work and can lead to a deeper understanding of the material.

Applying knowledge in practical scenarios involves:

- Recognizing the real-world relevance of your learning.
- Engaging in hands-on projects.
- Solving real-life problems.
- Seeking relevant work experiences.
- Teaching others.
- Reflecting on your learning.
- Being willing to experiment and learn from mistakes.

These activities not only reinforce what you've learned but also improve your ability to use your knowledge in a variety of contexts. By applying your knowledge, you can turn theoretical understanding into practical skills that you can use in your everyday life and career.

# CHAPTER 7

## ACCELERATING SKILL ACQUISITION

Acquiring new skills quickly is a valuable ability in today's fast-paced world. Whether learning for personal development, career advancement, or fun, picking up new skills efficiently can save you time and open up new opportunities. Several strategies can help you learn new skills more quickly.

Firstly, setting clear and specific goals is crucial. When you learn a new skill, be specific about what you want to achieve. Instead of a vague goal like "learn to play the piano," set a specific purpose like "learn to play 'Twinkle Twinkle Little Star' on the piano." Specific goals give you a clear target to work towards and make it easier to track your progress.

Breaking down the skill into smaller, manageable parts is another effective strategy.

Most skills consist of several smaller sub-skills. By breaking the talent down, you can focus on learning one part at a time, which is less overwhelming and more manageable. For example, if you're learning to code, start with basic syntax before moving on to more complex concepts.

Practicing regularly is critical to acquiring new skills quickly. The more you practice, the better you'll get. Try to set aside time every day to practice the new skill. Consistent practice helps reinforce your learning and speeds up the learning process.

Immersing yourself in a new skill can also speed up your learning. This means surrounding yourself with the talent as much as possible. If you're learning a new language, you might listen to music in that language, watch movies, or find conversation partners. Immersion helps you get used to the skill in different contexts and can make learning more natural and faster.

Learning from a variety of sources is another helpful strategy. Different sources can provide different perspectives and methods, deepening your understanding and exposing you to other aspects of the skill. For example, if you're learning to cook, you might watch cooking shows, read cookbooks, and take a cooking class.

Seeking feedback is also essential. Feedback helps you understand what you're doing well and what you need to improve. Try to get feedback from someone skilled in your learning area, whether it's a teacher, a mentor, or even a friend who knows about the subject. Constructive feedback can guide your practice and help you improve faster.

Another helpful strategy is to teach others what you're learning—leading forces you to organize and explain your knowledge clearly, which can deepen your understanding. Even if you're starting to learn the skill, trying to teach what you've learned so far can be a powerful way to reinforce your knowledge.

Finally, taking care of your physical and mental health is essential for quick learning. Adequate sleep, a healthy diet, regular exercise, and managing stress can all improve cognitive function, including your ability to learn new skills. When your body and mind are in good shape, you can better focus, retain information, and practice effectively.

Strategies for quickly acquiring new skills include:

- Setting clear and specific goals.
- Breaking the talent down into smaller parts.
- Practicing regularly.
- Immersing you in the craft.
- Learning from a variety of sources.
- Seeking feedback.
- Teaching others.
- Taking care of your physical and mental health.

Using these strategies makes the learning process more efficient and effective, allowing you to pick up new skills more quickly and easily.

## The role of practice and repetition

The role of practice and repetition in learning can't be overstated. It's the cornerstone of mastering any new skill or piece of knowledge. Practicing something repeatedly helps solidify that information in your mind, making it easier to recall when you need it.

Think of your brain as a muscle. Like muscles, your brain gets more robust and more efficient the more you use it. When you're learning something new, practicing it repeatedly helps strengthen the neural pathways in your brain. The more you use these pathways, the stronger and faster they become. This is why tricky things can become second nature after enough practice, like riding a bike or typing on a keyboard.

Repetition is essential when learning new information. When you first learn something, it's stored in your short-term memory, which is temporary and limited in capacity. However, when you review the information regularly, it starts to move into your long-term memory, which has a much larger capacity. This is why cramming for an exam often only works in the short term. You might remember the information for the test, but you're likely to forget it soon after. Regular review and repetition help transfer that knowledge to long-term memory, which can be accessed even years later.

Practice and repetition also play a crucial role in skill development. When you're learning a new skill, whether it's a physical skill like dancing or a mental skill like solving math problems, practice helps you improve. At first, you might find the skill difficult and have to think about every step. But as you practice, it becomes more automatic. This is because practice helps refine your technique and improve your efficiency, making the skill easier and more natural.

Another benefit of practice and repetition is that it helps build confidence. When you start learning something new, feeling unsure and hesitant is common. However, as you practice and see yourself improving, your confidence grows. This confidence can then motivate you to keep practicing and improving.

It's important to note that practice quality is as important as quantity. Mindlessly repeating something without paying attention could be more effective. Instead, your practice should be deliberate and focused. This means paying attention to what you're doing, noticing where you're making mistakes, and actively trying to improve. Deliberate practice can be more challenging and require more effort, but it's much more effective for learning.

Incorporating variety into your practice can also enhance its effectiveness. Doing the same thing in the same way every time can get boring, and when you're bored, you're less likely to be engaged and focused. Mixing up your practice routine can keep things interesting and help you stay committed. For example, if you're learning a language, you might mix up practicing speaking, writing, and listening. This variety can also help you apply the skill in different contexts, which is essential for real-world use.

Finally, regular breaks are an essential part of effective practice. This might seem counterintuitive, but frequent breaks can help you learn better. Taking a break gives your brain a chance to process and consolidate what you've learned. This is why studying for short periods with breaks in between is often more effective than looking for long periods without a break.

Practice and repetition are essential for learning and mastering new skills and information. They help strengthen neural pathways, transfer data to long-term memory, improve skill efficiency, build confidence, and make learning more enjoyable and effective. By practicing deliberately, incorporating variety, and taking regular breaks, you can maximize the benefits of practice and repetition in your knowledge.

# Overcoming plateaus in skill development

Overcoming plateaus in skill development is a common challenge many of us face when trying to improve in any area, whether learning a new language, mastering a musical instrument, or acquiring a professional skill. A plateau occurs when you reach a point where you no longer seem to be making progress despite regular practice and effort. It can be frustrating, but it's a normal part of the learning process, and there are strategies to overcome it.

Firstly, it's essential to recognize and accept the plateau. Realizing that plateaus are a normal part of learning can help you stay calm and focused rather than frustrated or discouraged. It's a sign that your initial rapid growth has leveled off and that it's time to adjust your approach.

One effective strategy for overcoming a plateau is to change up your routine. Doing the same practice routine or studying the same material in the same way can sometimes lead to stagnation. Changing your approach can challenge your brain in new ways, which can help reignite progress. For example, if you're learning a musical instrument and have hit a plateau, try playing different genres of music or experimenting with new techniques.

Setting new, more challenging goals can also help. If your current practice routine isn't pushing you enough, developing a more complex plan can provide the challenge to move past the plateau. These goals should be specific, achievable, and slightly outside your comfort zone. For instance, if you're learning a language, try setting a plan to have a conversation with a native speaker or to read a book in that language.

Another strategy is to focus on the finer details. Sometimes, a plateau occurs because you've mastered the basics and must focus on more advanced aspects of the skill. Paying attention to the skill's smaller, more intricate parts can help you continue to improve. For example, if you're a runner and you've plateau in your time, focusing on your running form or breathing technique can help you improve.

Seeking feedback from others can also be beneficial. An outside perspective can help you see things you might be missing. This feedback can come from a coach, teacher, mentor, friend, or colleague. They can offer insights and advice on improving and moving past your plateau.

Taking a break is another strategy that can be surprisingly effective. Sometimes, stepping away from the skill for a short period can help. This break can allow your brain to rest and process what you've learned. Often, you'll come back with a fresh perspective and renewed energy, which can help you overcome the plateau.

Cross-training or learning-related skills can also help. Developing skills in a related area can sometimes enhance your overall ability and help you break through the plateau. For example, if you're a writer whose hit a plateau, trying your hand at poetry or scriptwriting can give you new insights and ideas to help your writing.

Lastly, staying jovial and patient is crucial. Overcoming a plateau takes time and persistence. Staying positive and practicing is essential, even if you await immediate progress. With time and effort, you will eventually move past the plateau.

Overcoming plateaus in skill development involves:

- Recognizing the plateau.
- Changing your routine
- Setting new goals.
- Focusing on finer details.
- Seeking feedback.
- Taking breaks.
- Cross-training.
- Stay positive and patient.

Plateaus are a normal part of the learning process, and with the right strategies, you can overcome them and continue to improve and grow in your skills.

# CHAPTER 8

# UTILIZING TECHNOLOGY AND RESOURCES

In the modern world, technology has become a significant asset in learning. There's a wide array of technological tools and resources available that can enhance the learning experience, making it more interactive, accessible, and efficient. These tools cater to various learning styles and needs, and understanding what's available can help you make the most of them.

One of the most prominent resources is online courses and e-learning platforms. Websites like Courser, Udemy, and Khan Academy offer courses on almost every subject imaginable, taught by experts worldwide. These platforms often include video lectures, interactive quizzes, and forums where you can discuss the material with fellow learners. They're great for self-paced learning and offer the flexibility to learn anytime and anywhere.

Educational apps are another valuable resource. Many apps are designed to help with various aspects of learning. For language learning, apps like Duolingo and Babbel make learning a new language fun and engaging. For subjects like mathematics and science, apps like Wolfram Alpha and Photomath can help solve problems and explain concepts in an easy-to-understand manner. These apps often use gamification elements, which can make learning more enjoyable and less like a chore.

Interactive tools and simulations are handy for subjects that require practical understanding. For instance, websites like Codecademy for coding or Labster for science experiments offer interactive platforms where you can practice coding or conduct virtual lab experiments. These tools provide hands-on experience and a safe environment to practice and make mistakes.

Digital textbooks and online libraries are also valuable resources. Platforms like Google Books, Project Gutenberg, and various university websites offer a vast array of books and academic papers that you can access for free. Digital textbooks often have the added benefit of being more interactive and up-to-date than traditional textbooks.

Study aid tools like flashcard apps and note-taking software can also enhance learning. Flashcard apps like Anki or Quizlet are excellent for memorizing information, while note-taking tools like Evernote or Microsoft OneNote help organize your study materials effectively. These tools often come with features like syncing across devices, which means you can access your notes on your laptop, tablet, or phone, making studying more convenient.

Additionally, there are forums and online communities like Reddit or specific Facebook groups where you can find support, ask questions, and share resources. Being part of a learning community can provide motivation and additional insights.

Lastly, video conferencing tools like Zoom or Skype have become crucial, especially for remote learning and online classrooms. They allow real-time interaction with instructors and peers, making learning more collaborative and engaging.

Technological tools and resources for learning range from online courses, educational apps, interactive tools, digital textbooks, study aids, and online communities to video conferencing tools. These resources cater to different learning needs and styles, making education more accessible and engaging. By leveraging these tools, learners can enhance their study experience and gain new knowledge effectively and interactively.

## Online courses, apps, and other digital aids

Online courses, apps, and other digital aids have revolutionized how we learn today. They offer incredible resources at our fingertips, making learning more accessible, flexible, and often more engaging than traditional methods.

Starting with online courses, platforms like Coursera, Udemy, and Khan Academy have opened up a world of learning opportunities. They offer classes in everything from computer science to art history, taught by instructors from prestigious universities and institutions worldwide. What's great about these courses is that you can learn at your own pace. You can watch lectures at a time that suits you, pause and rewind if needed, and often access course materials like readings and quizzes to test your understanding.

Then there are educational apps, which have become a game-changer, especially for learning on the go. For instance, language learning apps like Duolingo make learning a new language fun, with interactive lessons that feel more like playing a game than sitting in a classroom. Math apps like Photomath let you scan math problems, give you the solution, and show you how to get there step-by-step. These apps are designed to be user-friendly and engaging, often using colorful graphics and interactive elements to motivate you.

Other digital aids include tools like note-taking apps and flashcard apps. Evernote, for example, allows you to take and organize notes across different devices, making it easy to keep track of your learning. Flashcard apps like Quizlet are great for memorizing facts, terms, or formulas. You can create your flashcards or use sets shared by other users. This can be particularly useful for subjects requiring much memorization, like language vocabulary or historical dates.

Interactive tools and simulations offer a unique way to learn complex concepts, especially in science and engineering. Websites that offer coding challenges, virtual labs, or math problem solvers provide hands-on experience in a way that a textbook can't. These tools are about giving you the correct answer and helping you understand the process and logic behind it.

Online libraries and resources have also become invaluable. Platforms like Google Scholar and various university websites give you access to countless academic papers, articles, and books. This is especially useful for research and in-depth study on specific topics. Plus, with digital formats, you have the advantage of easy searchability and accessibility.

Online communities and forums are another aspect of digital learning aids. Platforms like Reddit, Stack Exchange, or specific Facebook groups can be a treasure trove of information and support. You can ask questions, share resources, or just read through discussions on topics you're interested in. Sometimes, the tips and advice from these communities can provide practical insights not found in formal learning materials.

Lastly, video conferencing tools like Zoom or Microsoft Teams have become crucial, especially with the increase in remote learning and online classes. They allow real-time interaction and collaboration with teachers and peers, adding a personal touch to digital learning.

In summary, online courses, apps, and other digital aids provide a diverse and flexible approach to learning. They offer a variety of resources to suit different learning styles and needs, making education more accessible and engaging. Whether you're a student looking to supplement your studies, a professional wanting to upgrade your skills, or just a curious individual wishing to explore new areas of knowledge, these digital tools have something to offer.

## Leveraging social networks and communities for learning

Using social networks and online communities for learning is like tapping into a vast pool of knowledge and experience. These platforms offer more than just a way to stay connected with friends and family; they can be powerful tools for learning and personal development.

They provide access to diverse perspectives and resources that can enhance your learning experience.

One of the most significant advantages of social networks is connecting with experts and like-minded learners. Platforms like LinkedIn, for instance, allow you to follow and interact with professionals and thought leaders in your field of interest. You can gain insights from their posts, articles, and discussions, which can be incredibly valuable for learning and career development.

Online forums and communities like Reddit or Quora are great for asking questions and sharing knowledge. In these communities, people discuss various topics, from programming and design to history and science. You can ask specific questions, contribute your knowledge, or browse the discussions to learn from others' experiences and insights.

Facebook groups and Twitter chats can also be excellent learning resources. Many groups are dedicated to specific subjects or skills, and members often share helpful articles, videos, and tips. Twitter chats, usually organized around a hashtag, bring together people to discuss a particular topic at a set time. These can be great for learning about new trends, answering your questions, and connecting with people who share your interests.

YouTube is another powerful tool for learning. Beyond entertainment, it hosts a massive number of educational channels that cover practically every topic imaginable. Whether you're looking for tutorials, lectures, or documentary-style content, YouTube likely has something worthwhile. The comment sections can also be an excellent place to discuss the content with others and gain different perspectives.

Participating in webinars and live streams is another way to use digital platforms for learning. Many experts and organizations host webinars on a variety of topics, and these can be a great way to gain up-to-date knowledge and interact directly with the hosts and other participants.

Blogs and online articles are valuable learning resources often shared and discussed on social media. Following blogs related to your interests can provide steady information and ideas. Comment sections and social media shares often lead to discussions and additional insights.

It's essential, however, to approach information on social networks with a critical eye. Only some things you read online are accurate and trustworthy. Discerning credible sources and verifying information is a crucial skill when navigating these platforms.

In summary, leveraging social networks and online communities for learning involves connecting with the right people, engaging in meaningful discussions, and accessing various resources. These platforms can provide insights, perspectives, and information you might not easily find elsewhere. By actively participating and approaching information critically, you can significantly enhance your learning and stay updated in your field of interest.

# CHAPTER 9

# HEALTH, WELLNESS, AND LEARNING

Physical health dramatically affects how well you can learn and remember things. It's not just about not being sick; it's also about how you care for your body daily. When your body is healthy, your brain works better, making it easier to focus, understand, and remember.

What you eat matters a lot for learning. Foods that are good for your brain, like fruits, vegetables, nuts, and fish, can help you think clearly and concentrate better. But eating a lot of junk food and sugary snacks can make it harder for you to focus and learn.

Exercise is super important, too. Moving around and staying active helps blood flow to your brain, giving it the oxygen and nutrients it needs. Practise also makes you feel good because it releases chemicals in your brain that boost your mood and lower stress. This can make it easier for you to learn. Simple activities like walking, running, swimming, or even yoga can make a big difference.

Getting enough sleep is another big one. While asleep, your brain sorts through everything you learned during the day. If you don't get enough sleep, it can mess with your ability to concentrate and remember things. Most adults need about 7-9 hours of sleep each night to stay sharp.

Drinking enough water is essential, too. Even being slightly thirsty can make it harder to think and concentrate. Keeping hydrated helps keep your brain in top shape.

Dealing with stress is essential as well. Too much pressure can make it hard to learn new things. Doing stuff like meditating, breathing exercises, or regular physical activity can help keep your stress levels down.

Staying away from too much alcohol and drugs is also essential. These things can mess with how your brain works and make it harder to learn and remember things.

Lastly, regular check-ups with your doctor are a good idea. Some health issues, like diabetes or problems with your thyroid, can affect your brain and make learning more challenging. By keeping an eye on your health, you can ensure that nothing hinders your ability to learn.

So, looking after your physical health is essential for learning. Eating right, exercising, getting enough sleep, staying hydrated, managing stress, avoiding harmful substances, and keeping up with your health check-ups all help your brain work its best. By taking care of your body, you're also taking care of your brain, which means you can learn and remember things better.

## Importance of sleep, nutrition, and exercise

Sleep, nutrition, and exercise are the three pillars of good health. They are super essential not just for keeping your body healthy but also for your mind. Each one significantly affects how you feel daily and how well your brain works.

Let's start with sleep. Getting enough sleep is crucial. Your body and brain can rest and repair when you're asleep. It's like hitting the reset button. Good sleep helps you think clearer, concentrate better, and be more creative. It also helps with memory. Think about how you feel after a stormy night's sleep – you're probably groggy and find it hard to focus. Getting around 7-9 hours of sleep each night is recommended.

Next up is nutrition. What you eat has a significant impact on your health and how your brain functions. Eating a balanced diet with plenty of fruits, vegetables, whole grains, and lean proteins can give you the energy you need and help keep your brain sharp. These foods are packed with vitamins and minerals your brain needs to work well. On the other hand, too much junk food and sugar can make you feel sluggish and have a more challenging time concentrating.

Finally, there's exercise. Regular physical activity is excellent for your body and brain. Exercising increases blood flow, which means more oxygen and nutrients get to your brain. This can help improve your mood, make you more alert, and even improve your memory and thinking skills. It doesn't have to be anything intense – even a brisk walk, a bike ride, or a yoga session can do wonders.

So, sleep, nutrition, and exercise are super important for keeping your body and brain in top shape. They're not just about physical health;

they also play a significant role in how you think, feel, and handle stress. Taking care of these aspects of your health can help you feel better every day and boost your mental abilities.

## Stress management techniques for optimal learning

Handling stress is super important when you're trying to learn new things. When you're stressed out, it's a lot harder to focus and remember stuff. But the good news is that some simple ways to manage stress can help you learn better.

One of the best ways to deal with stress is to take breaks. Your brain can get tired when you're studying or working on something for a long time. Taking short breaks, even just a few minutes to stretch or walk, can help clear your head and reduce stress.

Another great technique is deep breathing or meditation. These practices help calm your mind and lower stress levels. You don't need much time for this – even just a few minutes of deep breathing or quiet meditation can make a big difference. There are lots of apps out there that can guide you through short meditation or breathing exercises.

Exercise is another excellent way to reduce stress. Physical activity releases chemicals in your brain that make you feel good and help lower pressure. It can be anything that gets you moving, like jogging, dancing, or even a brisk walk.

Talking to someone can also help with stress. Sometimes, sharing what's on your mind with a friend, family member, or counselor makes you feel much better. They might not be able to solve your problems, but just having someone listen can be helpful.

Staying organized can reduce stress, too. When you have a lot of things to do, it's easy to feel overwhelmed. But if you keep your study materials organized and make a plan for what you need to do, it can make things feel more manageable. A planner or a to-do list app can keep you on track.

Getting enough sleep is super important for managing stress. When you're tired, everything feels more arduous, and stress can worsen. Getting around 7-9 hours each night helps keep your stress levels down and makes it easier to focus and learn.

Lastly, finding time for fun and relaxation is crucial. It's important to balance work and study with activities that you enjoy. Whether hanging out with friends, watching a movie, or reading a book, doing things that make you happy is a great way to reduce stress.

Managing stress for optimal learning involves:

- Taking breaks.
- Practicing deep breathing or meditation.
- Exercising.
- Talking to someone.
- Staying organized.
- Getting enough sleep.
- Making time for fun and relaxation.

These techniques can help lower your stress levels, making focusing, learning, and remembering things easier. Remember, some stress is daily, but too much can make learning challenging, so finding ways to manage it can help.

# CHAPTER 10

# MASTERING THE ART OF FOCUS AND CONCENTRATION

Improving focus and minimizing distractions while learning is a lot like tuning a radio to get a clear signal. The clearer the signal, the better you can hear. Similarly, the more focused you are, the better you can learn. Here's how you can tune into your learning frequency without the static of distractions.

Having a special spot just for studying can make a huge difference. This should be a quiet place where you feel comfortable and can avoid interruptions. When you use this spot only for studying, your brain starts to link it to focus and hard work.

Sticking to a routine also helps. If you study at the same time every day, your brain gets used to concentrating during these times. It's like setting an internal clock that says, 'now it's time to focus.'

The Pomodoro Technique is another great tool. This means you study for 25 minutes, then take a five-minute break. These short bursts of study keep your mind fresh and focused. During your breaks, it's good to step away from your desk to really give your brain a rest.

In today's world, phones and the internet can be a big distraction. Try turning off your notifications or using apps that block distracting websites when you're studying. If you don't need the internet, maybe even switch off your WiFi.

Having all your study materials ready before you start can also prevent your mind from wandering. This way, you don't have to keep getting up to find things, which can break your concentration.

Practices like mindfulness or meditation can train your brain to focus better. Even a few minutes each day can help improve your concentration and mental clarity.

Before you start a study session, setting a clear goal for what you want to achieve can keep you on track. Knowing exactly what you need to do keeps your study sessions purposeful.

Simple exercises like focusing on your breathing can also help improve your concentration. These can be done for a few minutes daily and help train your brain to focus.

Your physical health is important too. Regular exercise, good sleep, and eating right are all key to staying focused. Exercise, especially, can help sharpen your brain.

Lastly, some people find that certain sounds, like soft music or white noise, can help block out distracting noises. This can create a bubble of concentration, making it easier to focus.

By using these techniques, you can build a strong radio signal for your brain, making it easier to tune into the task at hand and block out the static of distractions. Remember, it's all about finding what works best for you and sticking to it.

## Importance of a conducive learning environment

Creating the right environment for learning is super important. It's like setting the stage before a big performance. The right setting can make a huge difference in how well you learn and remember things. A conducive learning environment is one that makes you feel comfortable and helps you focus without too many distractions.

First, think about the physical space where you're learning. It should be somewhere quiet where you won't be disturbed too often. This could be a corner of your room, a desk in the library, or even a quiet café. The key is to find a spot where you can settle in and not be constantly interrupted.

Lighting is another thing to consider. Good lighting can reduce eye strain and help keep you alert. Natural light is great, but if that's not possible, make sure you have enough bright, artificial light to see your materials clearly.

Your comfort is also important. A comfortable chair and a desk at the right height can prevent aches and pains. If you're uncomfortable, you'll likely find it hard to focus for long periods. But remember, too comfortable might make you sleepy. So, find a balance where you're comfortable enough to focus but not so cozy that you want to take a nap.

Then there's the noise level. Some people need complete silence to concentrate, while others work better with a bit of background noise. If you're easily distracted by noise, consider using earplugs or noise-canceling headphones. If you like a bit of sound, soft background music or ambient sounds can create a pleasant environment without being too distracting.

Organizing your study materials is also key. Keep your study space tidy and have all your materials like books, notes, and stationery organized and within reach. A cluttered desk can make your mind feel just as cluttered.

Another part of a conducive learning environment is the digital space. If you're studying on a computer, try to keep your digital workspace as organized as your physical one. Close tabs you don't need and keep your files and folders well-organized. This can help reduce digital clutter, which can be just as distracting as physical clutter.

Lastly, the right environment isn't just about the physical and digital space. It's also about creating the right mental space. This means setting aside specific times for studying and trying to stick to a routine. It also means being in the right mindset, where you're ready to focus and learn.

In summary, a conducive learning environment is a combination of the right physical space, comfortable furniture, good lighting, an appropriate noise level, organized materials, and a focused mindset. By creating this kind of environment, you can help make your learning more effective and enjoyable. Remember, what works best can vary from person to person, so it's all about finding what works best for you.

## Exercises and habits to enhance concentration for effective learning

Boosting your concentration can really help you learn better. It's like turning up the volume on your favorite song so you can hear it more clearly. There are some exercises and habits you can start doing that can make a big difference in how well you can focus.

First, it's good to get into the habit of taking short breaks while you're studying. Studying for hours on end can make you tired and your mind might start to wander. Taking a quick break every now and then, like a short walk or just stepping outside for a few minutes, can refresh your mind and help you focus better when you get back to work.

Mindfulness exercises are really useful too. These are exercises where you focus on being in the moment, like paying attention to your breath or what you can hear around you. Doing this for just a few minutes each day can train your brain to focus better. It's like doing a workout, but for your brain.

Another good habit is to set specific goals for each study session. Instead of just sitting down to 'study,' decide what you want to achieve in that session. Maybe it's to understand a certain topic or to finish a set of problems. Having a clear goal can keep your study sessions on track and help you stay focused.

Staying organized can also help with concentration. If your study area is messy and your notes are all over the place, it's easy to get distracted. Keeping your space tidy and your materials organized can make it easier to focus on what you're trying to learn.

Physical exercise is great for concentration too. Regular exercise, even something as simple as a daily walk, can help improve your focus and concentration. It gets your blood flowing and can help clear your head.

Eating right is important as well. Foods like fruits, vegetables, nuts, and fish are great for your brain and can help improve your concentration. Try to avoid too much sugar or junk food, especially right before you need to study.

Getting enough sleep is super important. When you're tired, it's much harder to concentrate. Most adults need about 7-9 hours of sleep each night to feel their best.

Finally, try to reduce distractions as much as you can. This might mean turning off your phone or using apps that block distracting websites when you're studying. The less you have competing for your attention, the easier it is to concentrate on what you're learning.

In summary, improving your concentration involves taking regular breaks, practicing mindfulness, setting specific goals, staying organized, exercising regularly, eating healthy foods, getting enough sleep, and reducing distractions. By working on these habits and exercises, you can improve your ability to focus, which can make your learning more effective and enjoyable. Remember, it takes time to build these habits, but with practice, they can really help boost your concentration.

## The role of mindfulness and mental clarity in maintaining consistent focus

Mindfulness and mental clarity play a big role in helping you keep your focus steady. When you're mindful, you're really paying attention to what's happening right now. You're not worrying about what happened yesterday or what you need to do tomorrow. This kind of focus is super helpful when you're trying to learn or get work done.

Think about when your mind is all over the place. It's hard to focus on anything, right? But when you're clear-headed and calm, it's a lot easier to concentrate. Mindfulness helps you get to that calm, clear-headed state. It's like it clears away the mental clutter, so you can focus on what's in front of you.

You can practice mindfulness in simple ways. One way is to take a few minutes each day to just sit quietly and focus on your breathing. When your mind starts to wander, you gently bring it back to your breath. This practice can help train your brain to stay focused.

Another way to use mindfulness is to really pay attention to what you're doing at the moment. For example, when you're studying, try to focus just on that. If you start thinking about something else, gently bring your attention back to your studying. It's not about never getting distracted – it's about noticing when you do and bringing your focus back.

Having mental clarity is also about taking care of your overall well-being. Things like getting enough sleep, eating healthy, and getting some exercise can help keep your mind clear. When your body feels good, your mind usually does too.

Using mindfulness and working towards mental clarity is kind of like training a muscle. The more you do it, the stronger it gets. Over time, you'll probably find it gets easier to focus and stay concentrated for longer periods. This can be a big help in all kinds of situations, whether you're studying, working, or just trying to get better at a hobby.

So, in short, mindfulness and mental clarity are all about being in the moment and keeping your mind clear. They can help you focus better and make your learning or work more efficient and enjoyable. It takes some practice, but it's worth it for how much it can help improve your focus.

# CHAPTER 11

## PUTTING IT ALL TOGETHER

Creating a personalized 48-hour learning plan is a great way to tackle a new topic or skill in a short amount of time. This focused, intensive learning can be effective if you plan it right. The idea is to make a plan that suits your learning style and fits into your schedule, helping you make the most of the limited time.

First, pick what you want to learn and set a clear goal. What do you want to achieve in these 48 hours? You may want to get the basics of a new language, understand the fundamentals of a coding language, or learn how to use a new software tool. Having a specific goal will guide your learning and help you stay focused.

Next, break down your goal into smaller, manageable tasks. If you're learning a new language, these tasks include learning common phrases, basic grammar rules, and numbers. For coding, it might be understanding basic syntax, writing simple programmers, and learning about basic data structures. Breaking it down like this makes it less overwhelming and gives you a clear roadmap.

Then, plan out your 48 hours. Decide how much time you'll dedicate to each task and when to work on them. Be realistic about how much time you can focus and learn effectively. It's usually better to have several shorter study sessions with breaks in between rather than one long marathon session. Schedule breaks to rest and recharge - as important as the study time.

Choose the right resources for your learning. This might include online courses, tutorial videos, books, or apps. Pick resources that match your learning style. If you learn better by watching, find videos or courses. If you prefer reading, look for articles or books. Also, think about practical resources like flashcards or practice exercises.

During your 48-hour learning sprint, it's crucial to stay flexible. Adjust your plan if you find a particular task is taking longer than expected. Consider spending less time on a job that you grasp quickly and more on one that's giving you trouble.

It's also helpful to reflect on what you're learning as you go. After each session, think about what you learned, what you found easy or challenging, and how it fits into your overall goal. This reflection can help reinforce what you've learned and give you insights into how you know best.

Lastly, review what you've learned at the end of the 48 hours and think about your next steps. Did you reach your goal? What areas do you need to focus on more? Planning your next steps, whether continuing to learn the topic or moving on to something else, can help keep the momentum going.

Creating a personalized 48-hour learning plan involves:

- Setting a clear goal.
- Breaking it down into manageable tasks.
- Planning out your time.
- Choosing the right resources.
- Staying flexible.
- Reflecting on your learning.
- Review your progress at the end.

This focused approach can help you quickly grasp a new topic or skill and maximize your limited time.

## Case studies and examples

Using case studies and examples is a powerful way to learn new things. They show you how the stuff you're teaching works in real life, making it easier to understand and remember. Let's say you're learning about business management. Reading about theories and strategies is one thing, but looking at a case study of a successful company and how it handled a challenging situation can bring those theories to life. You get to see how the decisions were made, what worked, and sometimes what didn't. This can help you think about how to apply those lessons in your life or work.

Examples are just as helpful. They are like mini case studies and can be found in almost any subject. For example, seeing many examples of how to solve a particular problem can make it much more straightforward if you're learning math. Understanding the formula is one thing, but seeing the procedure used in several examples helps you see the pattern and get the hang of it.

In science subjects, examples and case studies can show how scientific principles are used in the real world. Let's say you're learning about renewable energy. A case study on a city that uses solar panels can show you how solar power works on a large scale, the benefits, and the challenges they might have faced.

In subjects like history or sociology, case studies, and examples can help you understand complex events or social phenomena. For example, studying a particular historical event, like the Civil Rights Movement, through detailed examples and stories can give you a much deeper understanding than just reading about dates and facts.

What's excellent about case studies and examples is that they make learning more enjoyable. It's like adding color to a black-and-white picture. They can provide context and make the material more relatable. Sometimes, they can be inspiring, like reading about someone who overcame considerable challenges to achieve something unique.

Case studies and examples are helpful in learning because they show how theories and concepts are applied in real life. They can make complex ideas clearer, help you remember things better, and make learning more enjoyable. No matter what you're studying, looking for case studies and examples can significantly deepen your understanding.

## Encouragement and advice for continued learning and growth

Learning and growing is one of the best things you can do for yourself. It keeps your mind sharp, opens up new opportunities, and can be satisfying. But it can be challenging. There might be times when you feel like you need more motivation. Remember that it's okay to take a break and recharge during these times. Learning is not a race, and it's essential to go at a pace that works for you.

One of the best advice for continuous learning is to stay curious. Try to see learning not just as a task but as an adventure. Be curious about the world, ask questions, and explore new ideas. This can make learning more enjoyable and less of a chore. Don't be afraid to try new things. Sticking with what you know is easy, but stepping out of your comfort zone can be rewarding. You might discover a new passion or find you're good at something you never expected. And even if it doesn't work out, you'll have learned something valuable.

Another key to continued learning is to set realistic goals. It's great to be ambitious, but setting too high goals can be discouraging. Break your goals down into smaller steps that you can manage. Celebrate your progress along the way. This can keep you motivated and make the learning process more rewarding.

Remember, it's okay to ask for help. Nobody knows everything, and sometimes you need a little guidance. Be bold about asking for help from teachers, mentors, friends, or online communities. People are often more willing to help than you think. Finding a learning community can also be a big help. Whether it's a study group, an online forum, or a class, being around others, learning can be motivating. You can share tips, support, and learn from each other's experiences. Lastly, be kind to yourself. Learning is a journey with ups and downs. Sometimes, you must progress, but that's part of the process. Don't beat yourself up. Just keep going, and you'll get there.

To continue learning and growing, stay curious, try new things, set realistic goals, don't be afraid to ask for help, find a learning community, and be kind to yourself. Remember, the journey of learning is as important as the destination. Each step you take is an achievement and brings you closer to your goals. Keep going, and you'll be amazed at how much you can achieve.

Printed in Great Britain
by Amazon